The Questions
of
Mary

Other Books By James Galluzzo

The New Eden Series:
The Sacred Feminine
Sacred Masculine
The Merge: A Reemerging of the Sacred Feminine
and Sacred Masculine
A Spiritual Handbook: A Resource for Travelers
and Guides on the Journey
The Spirituality of Mary Magdalene
Jesus as Liberator and the Gospel Values
Quotes and Reflection Questions for Journaling
Your Spiritual Journey
Spiritual Writing: Be the Author of Your Own
Story
Stop Whining, Choose Life

The Questions of Mary

Reflections on Mary Magdalene

BY JAMES GALLUZZO

Gray Wings Press, LLC
Milwaukie, Oregon
2015

gray wings press

Library of Congress Control Number: 2015950398

ISBN 978-0692496497
0692496491

A NEW STORY WILL BE TOLD WHEN WE ASK QUESTIONS, REFLECT ON THEM AND ANSWER THEM. THIS LEADS TO DISCOVERY, GROWTH AND MOVEMENT, AND THEN A NEW STORY EMERGES

Acknowledgments

Cover Painting by Marianne Manning
The painting portrays Mary Magdalene as a woman
who reads and writes. The skull represents the
message of Jesus that Mary is chosen to spread
after his death.

Cover Design by Karen Gatens
Gatens Design

Special thanks to those who helped with
this book:
Sue Hammond,
Annie Doyle
Vickie Rooks
Sheree Tuppen
Kathy Fanning
Mary Gonzales
Ann Faricy
Maggie Stopka

❧ PREFACE ❧

Mary Magdalene journeyed beside Jesus deep in conversation. Jesus respected her as a primary confidant. She had the authority to speak to Jesus, receive his command and teach his message to other disciples. She was faithful to Jesus. She was at his side through his ministry. She bore witness to his crucifixion and death, and his resurrection. She continued to be loyal to him after he was gone. This intimacy with Jesus two thousand years ago enabled Mary Magdalene to write two books, her apocryphal *Gospel of Mary Magdalene* discovered in 1896 and her *Questions of Mary* referenced in only a few writings by others but never found, some think destroyed.

The prominence of Mary Magdalene as a gifted woman central to the meaning of Jesus was re-established in the Western world when I was a young man. In my next forty years as an educator, scholar and priest, I studied Mary Magdalene. I was devoted to knowing her. I wondered about her curiosity with Jesus. In 2008, I wrote *The Spirituality of Mary Magdalene*. Now, I recreate her lost writings in the *Questions of Mary*. In this latest book I ask the questions that I believe Mary Magdalene would have asked Jesus, and I answer as Jesus would have spoken. I rely on Mary Magdalene's own words from her gospel and the message of Jesus found in the four gospels and the Gnostic gospels, among other sources of published and spiritual works.

My *Questions of Mary* is Mary Magdalene's two-thousand-year-old story, and it is today's story. It takes us out of our limbo, what Thomas Berry described as the world between two stories, the old one about creation and the start of humankind and the new one not yet known, one that speaks to us today. The new story is told here as Mary Magdalene first perceived what is true and the foundation of her spiritual message received from her conversations with Jesus.

Much has been written about Mary Magdalene. Her name appears over a dozen times in the four Canonical gospels. The Gnostic gospels mention her several times. Art and music feature her. The institutional church has dealt with her in many contradictory ways. It has made her a saint, prolonged misinformation about her, discredited her, and failed to honor her rich spiritual gifts and to recognize her role in the early church. What is missing from these other works about Mary Magdalene is her message and the foundation of her spirituality, the human longing for truth. Her themes of being fully human, our responsibility for spiritual growth, God within and God Among and challenges regarding dualism, set the tone for her story. I capture the essence of Mary Magdalene in this book using 52 quotes, each with a question and answer. My suggested practice for you, as I have done, is to meditate and reflect on one quote for each week of the year and then think of how you might answer the question.

❧ Mary Magdalene ❧

Let me first tell you who the real Mary Magdalene is. Mary Magdalene touches the whole of Western Civilization. She is an honored saint, woman and a teacher of deep devotion. She is a misunderstood woman who challenged the fears of men and the failures of institutions and religions. Mary Magdalene has endured, her character reinvented from friend and foe, follower of Jesus, lover, prostitute, feminine icon, witness, preacher, mystic and saint.

Traditions of the New Testament gospels, early church fathers, Western European Church and the Eastern Orthodox Church convey a variety of messages about Mary Magdalene. The many traditions have different levels of acceptance of Mary Magdalene. An oversimplified Western and patriarchal mindset prevailed for centuries to cast her a poor reputation, uncorrected until the mid- 1900s.

Passages about Mary Magdalene in the canonical gospels and other texts show her as a prominent disciple and forbearer of the resurrection of Jesus. The study of the *Gospel of Mary of Magdalene* shows Mary Magdalene's empowerment by Jesus. Mary Magdalene was a strong and caring leader to the disciples. This is one way she displayed the authority Jesus gave her. She was an active character in Jesus' ministry and at his crucifixion, burial and empty tomb. The tradition of the New Testament believes her to be a devoted follower of Jesus. She is faithful, loyal, courageous and a positive light.

Pope Gregory the Great wrote in the sixth century that Jesus heralded to a woman on Easter day, "Proclaim to my disciples the mysteries you have seen. Become the first teacher of the teachers. Peter, who has denied me, must learn that I can also choose women as apostles."[1]

The Western European tradition historically presented false ideas of Mary Magdalene's character. In art and literature, Mary Magdalene is portrayed as a prostitute, the Christian model of a female redeemed. This image of the forgiven prostitute is a mistaken assumption. *The New Catholic Encyclopedia* remarks, "It is more difficult to understand how the repentant sinner was identified as Mary Magdalene by Gregory the Great in 591, since St. Luke introduces Mary by name immediately after finishing the story of the penitent woman, whose name he either does not know or wishes not to reveal."[2]

---

[1]*Pope Gregory the Great, Homily XXXIII.*
[2]*The New Catholic Encyclopedia*

It was not until 1969 that the Catholic Church finally admitted Mary Magdalene was not a prostitute, thus releasing her real image. In 2006, Pope John Paul II proclaimed the tradition of Mary of Magdalene, as apostle to the apostles. He said she was a biblical saint, an apostle and a woman who spoke with authority about what she knew of the suffering and pain of life.

Eastern Orthodox tradition is truer to the gospel tradition. They had the intelligence to see her identity as different from the other Marys—Mary of Bethany and the "sinful" woman. They recognized Mary Magdalene as the apostle to the apostles, the one who stands in the presence of the risen Jesus and tells the male disciples the news of the resurrection.

Mary Magdalene is important as the first person to preach the "good news of the resurrection to the other disciples" in the *Gospel of John*. The *Gospel of John* affirms that Jesus was the one who honored her with the position to do so.

The disciples present a view of Mary Magdalene as an active follower and witness to the resurrection. Many hold that the role of Mary Magdalene was weakened by the patriarchy of early church leaders. One of the earliest examples of this is in the *Gospel of Peter* when he says Mary Magdalene was just one of the women who came to the empty tomb and when she saw a man in white robes she left in fear. Then Peter proclaims he was the first witness to the resurrection. The *Gospel of Thomas* talks about the competition between Mary Magdalene and Peter and the special relationship Mary Magdalene had with Jesus that made Peter jealous.

The gospels are not the only place where Mary Magdalene is seen as a close follower and witness. Numerous other documents include: *Gospel of Peter, Acts of Peter, Acts of Paul, Gospel of Philip, Acts of Philip, First Apocalypse of James, Gospel of Thomas, Pistis Sophia, Sophia of Jesus Christ, Dialogue of the Savior, Gospel of the Egyptians, Questions of Mary and Gospel of Mary Magdalene.*

Some specific examples occur in the *Pistis Sophia.* Mary Magdalene is portrayed as a "questioner" who asks 39 of the 64 questions when Jesus is teaching his disciples. Also in the *Pistis Sophia,* Mary Magdalene is called blessed and had her heart more focused on the kingdom of heaven rather than on fear.

The *Gospel of Thomas* and the *Pistis Sophia* talk about Mary Magdalene as having a loving and strong relationship with Jesus. The *Gospel of Philip* says that Mary Magdalene was the most beloved disciple and was continually with Jesus. She is often named as Jesus' companion and that Jesus loved her more than all the other disciples.

First Apocalypse of James, points out that, "James should turn to Mary and the other women for instruction." The *Gospel of Thomas* also shows strong leadership qualities of Mary Magdalene.

Sophia of Jesus Christ and the *Dialogue of the Savior*, follow the tradition of her asking questions of Jesus. In both narratives, she is mentioned by name as being given the blessing to teach and the authority to speak to Jesus. The *Questions of Mary* is associated with the *Pistis Sophia*. Jesus gave Mary Magdalene a revelation that comes in the form of questions. Mary, Levi, Andrew and Peter were called by Jesus to ask questions to better understand his message. Mary led the leadership in this and recorded the questions and answers.

Mary Magdalene begins her gospel describing Jesus teaching his disciples. The dialogue takes place through a series of questions. The section contains four characters: Levi, Andrew, Peter, and Mary Magdalene. Mary Magdalene's gospel creates an understanding of the deep bond that the disciples had with Jesus. It ends with Mary Magdalene stepping into a leadership position. Mary Magdalene comforts them and turns their hearts toward the good news of Jesus. She is seen as a spiritual leader in the *Gospel of John* and the *Gospel of Mary*. Both gospels say in similar words, "Let not your hearts be troubled" and Jesus and Mary Magdalene offer peace to the disciples.

The second part of her gospel includes a special message Mary Magdalene received from Jesus and shares. Peter, Andrew, Levi and Mary discuss what following Jesus would mean after his death and resurrection. Mary Magdalene shows great wisdom but Andrew says, "These teachings are strange." Peter questions whether Jesus really said these things to a woman, when Jesus did not tell the male disciples. Levi challenges Peter for dismissing this woman and admits that Jesus loved her more than the others.

Mary Magdalene's gospel tells people that every person experiences the "God Within" if they are open and available to true "inner knowing", to see a deeper and clearer way of developing a deep spiritual connection.

James Galluzzo, *The Spirituality of Mary Magdalene*

1. Why the talk about the God Within, instead of some God in the sky?

It is within each one of us that the Divine dwells. We need to look within to find the Divine rather than look to a guru or institution; we have the answer inside ourselves. This is called inner knowing. Others can help with support, teaching or answers to our questions, but we have to embrace the inner knowledge.

We are all on the journey and life is about going on the journey, not the getting there. It is in the seeking, questioning and dreaming in our inner knowledge that we will find the Divine and find what is holy. This is how we will discover a way, a truth and a light.

If we use the English or Greek word meaning NEAR, the implication is that the Kingdom of God is some time in the future, not yet here. Yet the Hebrew word KARAV means the exact opposite. It gives us the meaning:
"IT IS HERE! IT HAS ARRIVED!"
The Kingdom of Heaven or the Kingdom of God is always present tense. It is NOW.
The Evangelical Orthodox Church

2. Is this why the Kingdom is at hand?

Yes. Too many people think life is about coping and surviving and then we die and hopefully go to heaven. But heaven is not in the future only. It is both now and not yet. There are graced moments in our lives and they are all around us if we would take time to notice. Everything is holy and we get to discover the grace every day in our lives.

Beauty sees the goodness in everything, the light and darkness, the body and soul, heaven and earth, man and women.
James Galluzzo

3. Why contradict the current and ancient idea of dualism?

The message I want to hold out is our deep connection to one another and to all things. Beauty unites. Dualism separates. The idea of dualism begins with separation: spirit and body, heaven and earth, masculine and feminine, adult and child, God and humans, upper class and lower class. The separation is a disconnect in itself, but when the separation leads to conflicts and the conflicts lead to one being superior to the other, then a hierarchical model takes over. One is viewed as better than, with power over, more powerful than, which can produce disdain or lack of respect for the other. This breaks the hope of being one, of working together to honor all of creation. The message I want to hold out is our deep connection to one another and to all things.

Mary invites people to free themselves from dualism—no more body or soul, heaven or earth, male or female, night or day, darkness or light, all are whole and complete and are connected.

James Galluzzo, *The Spirituality of Mary Magdalene*

4. How do we live free of the dualism that pervades our society?

It starts with believing in "both/and" not "either/or." Only when we free ourselves from this concept can we be whole and embrace the female and male, body and soul, heart and mind, human and divine energy. Then strength, creativity, intelligence, gentleness and power will be one. Then each of us will find peace, love, compassion, justice, forgiveness, healing and connection.

The challenge will be to respect the earth and the body. We must cherish creation, and we must be intimate with our body, mind, heart and soul. This will allow us to see the humanity in all people and the holiness in all people and all creation.

Nothing exists in itself or by itself.
The Gospel of Mary Magdalene

5. What about the Divine among?

The Divine is a living force who wants to communicate with humans. The Divine wants the invisible and the visible to be one and wants the worlds of spirit and body to be one. When two or three are gathered, it is a holy event. This shows the power of community, being in communion.

We are to be models of two becoming one, the feminine and masculine becoming sacred. We both have to hold forth the inner knowing in one another. We both have to be one body and one spirit. And then, when we gather together, it is both holy and whole.

*Do not lay down any rules beyond what
I appointed you and do not give a law
like the lawgiver lest you be
constrained by it.*
The Gospel of Mary Magdalene Chapter 5, vs. 38

6. Where is the place for laws in ministry?

There is no need for outside laws; the truth
resides inside of each of us. We are to love, and all
laws and prophecies are based on the love of self,
others, and the transcendental. If regulations, dogma
or teachings are not based on love, then they are
false teachings.

Theologians may quarrel,
but the mystics of the world
speak the same language.
Meister Eckhart

7. Do we all have mystical experiences?

When people see the truth and write about it, speak it and teach it, they experience the mystical. They experience the inner revelation. They will see, hear and understand the Divine because they honored the fact that being fully human means one can see, hear, think, feel, act and decide. This is why people understand the Divine among and then see the Divine in others. People are mystics because they see the holy in the ordinary.

No, no!

The adventures and stories first,
explanations take such a dreadful time
Lewis Carroll, *Alice's Adventures in Wonderland*

8. Why tell stories instead of clearly writing down the message?

Stories hold all the sacred knowledge. Divine knowledge is not outside people; it is in our story. Connection is the integration of human stories. The world is a vast tapestry of stories that hold all things. When we are in right relationship and listen to the whole of the cosmos and each other's story, we are connecting, we are "godding".

The best and most beautiful things in the world cannot be seen or even touched—they must be felt with the heart.

Helen Keller

9. Why talk about the heart so much?

The heart does not get enough attention.

We must follow our heart, lift up our heart and tell our good news story. Our truth and our stories reside in our hearts, minds, souls and bodies.

The Divine lives in our hearts, body, mind and soul. The Divine speaks to us through every part of us. Therefore we have the opportunity to be at one with all of our self. We must listen to our hearts.

One's philosophy is not best expressed
in words; it is expressed in the choices
one makes . . . and the choices we make
are ultimately our responsibility.

Eleanor Roosevelt

10. What is meant by our personal responsibility?

When we allow the Divine to be in our hearts, to birth, to grow, and take root in us, then we will be in presence with the spirit which will aid us on our journey to wholeness.

It is a choice, and it is our responsibility to make it happen. It means being open, listening to our hearts, seeking knowledge. We cannot expect a blind faith that comes from above. It is not faith alone or following what institutions tell us we have to do. We have a heart, body, soul and mind. We are each responsible to be in touch with our entire self. We are in a human covenant, a heart-to-heart agreement with our inherent nature, which enables and requires us to be responsible for our choices and the well being of others.

It is about people, not poverty.
It is about community, not buildings.
It is about listening, not speaking.
It is about modeling, not making laws.
It is about love, not dogma. It is about
following our heart, not a creed.
James Galluzzo

11. Why not form a church and set up a new religion?

That is what people want us to do. Is that what should happen? The church will come into being later, and when it does there will be great fear that the message will become institutionalized, will become a set of dogmas and become barren ritual rather than celebrating life and feeding people. Many previous religions lost the core of the message through politics, corruption and dogmas that contradicted their core principles.

We are not to teach about dogma, formulas, creeds, rules and regulations. We are to form a community that is about love, about loving God with heart, soul, mind and body and loving our neighbor as we love ourselves.

People are trying to make it more, make it complicated. But everything that matters to me, the laws, the prophets, the psalms, the stories, and what will be written will have to be grounded in love. I am afraid people will get distracted from the loving.

People will keep reminding others who love to stay focused on loving.

Maybe even our followers will fight about what is true and try to create a language, a creed, a structure that will separate people, keep people rigid and prevent people from growing along their spiritual journey.

We must not generate more precepts masquerading as holy. We do not want to set a belief system in stone that can't breathe. We need to build a community about life and love and living abundantly.

Seven Deadly Sins
Wealth without work,
Pleasure without conscience,
Science without humanity,
Knowledge without character,
Politics without principle,
Commerce without morality,
Worship without sacrifice.
Mahatma Gandhi

12. What is all this talk about sin?

Sin does not exist in itself. It is not an outside force called evil. It is not "the devil that makes people do it." If that were true, people would be removed from responsibility, from free choice and from clear thinking. Unfortunately we make choices that disconnect us from our authentic selves. This happens when we do not follow our hearts. We are all called to be in harmony with ourselves, others and nature. When we are not being true to our nature, there is disharmony.

Male and female represent the two sides of the great radical dualism. But in fact they are perpetually passing into one another. Fluid hardens to solid, solid rushes to fluid. There is no wholly masculine man, no purely feminine woman.

Margaret Fuller

13. How can women be among the followers when it is so culturally radical?

We must break the cultural barrier against women, to see women treated with dignity and respect and be seen as people of worth.

Mary is a first example of women freely choosing to follow me. She is called a disciple, even an apostle. John will call her the apostle of apostles. She has broken the cultural barriers by learning to read and write, which goes against the teaching of the Scribes and Pharisees.

She is an energetic, impulsive, caring, intelligent woman. She has been faithful to our ministry and has contributed to the needs of our followers. She has been present to my living, will be present to my suffering and dying and will be the first to experience the new life that is held out for all people.

She will help women see themselves as equal reflections of God's image.

I am afraid of Peter because he threatens me and hates our gender and hates our race... When Mary finished saying these things, the savior marveled greatly at the answers she gave, for she had become entirely pure spirit. Jesus answered and said to her, "Well done, Mary, pure spiritual woman. This is the interpretation of the word".

Pistis Sophia

14. Others say that Mary is a prostitute, a rebel, a sinner, a liberated woman, a lover and a wife. Others are jealous of our time together and of our relationship. Who does Jesus say Mary is?

She is a heart-warming example of thankful openness in living and loving. She taught me what friendship and love is all about. Her openness has freed people from the distraction and temptations that get in the way of being fully human. In so many ways, she has acted on the appreciation and the freedom relationship has offered. Her freedom will allow her to stand by me when others abandon or reject me, when I am ridiculed, beaten and killed. She will be the first to realize my gift was not offering my life, but my gift was giving new life. She sees clearly that I was about life and living abundantly so that others may choose to do the same.

She had coveted with earthly eyes, but now through penitence these are consumed with tears. She had spoken proud of things with her mouth, but in kissing the Lord's feet, she now planted her mouth on the Redeemer's feet. For every delight, therefore, she now immolated herself. She turned the mass of her crimes to virtue, in order to serve God entirely in penance, for as much as she had wrongly held God in contempt.

Pope Gregory the Great, *Homily XXXIII on Luke 7*

15. Why is anointing so important?

It was important for the scribes, the priests, and the Pharisees to see that a woman and a faithful follower would recognize that I needed to be anointed for my ministry. It is to be a call of the people, not a call from a king or someone in authority.

Mary so graciously brought an alabaster jar of

perfume and washed my feet with her tears and dried them with her beautiful hair and then anointed me with holy perfume.

Remember how the Pharisees were so upset and ridiculed me for letting a woman touch me, especially a strong, impulsive woman, who didn't listen to authority figures and was outspoken and did not follow the rules of how women should act!

The Divine's plan is for anointing to come upon those who are trustworthy and to let them know they will do great things for the world.

James Galluzzo

16. What was the purpose in letting me wash your feet?

When I came into their house, no one gave me water for my feet, but Mary wet my feet with her tears and wiped them with her hair. No one greeted me, but she gave me a kiss. No one put oil on my head, but she poured her special and expensive perfume on my feet. She loved so much. People will remember her loving and kind gesture and others will do this in memory of her and of me.

As a woman, she continued the great tradition of Samuel who took a flask of oil and poured it on Saul's head and kissed him and anointed Saul as leader of God's people. She continued the tradition of Samuel who poured the oil and anointed David, and then the Spirit came upon him.

Mary's perfume was like the oil used to anoint the pillar, it was olive oil of the finest grade of purity. It was expensive, used to show the high value placed on the anointed object or person.

In Genesis, Jacob shows the greatest respect for the place where he met with God by pouring oil over it.

Her gesture showed respect for my ministry and me, challenged me to be all that I could be, to be faithful to my call.

*I am not a Savior or a Redeemer.
I am a Reminder. I am here to remind
people to grow in wisdom and
knowledge, to love God and our
neighbor as our self, to follow our
hearts, to stay on the right track of
peace and justice and to be human.*
James Galluzzo

17. If God will never forsake us, why do we need you to save us?

I never said I came to save anybody. Why would I need to save anyone?

God will never forsake anyone; he loves us all unconditionally, no matter what we do. So if we believe that God will never abandon us, then we were never lost, and we don't need to be saved. The whole idea of needing to be saved by something outside us, like a religion or institution, disempowers people.

*I came to offer new life, to encourage
people to live life fully, to be all they
are called to be and to live in
abundance and not in scarcity.*
James Galluzzo

18. Well then, why did Jesus come?

That is unfolding for me, but I do know that I
came as a human to remind people to be human. So I
would say, I came as a reminder, not as a savior. I
want to live my life modeling humanity, showing
what it means to be human and reminding everyone
to be fully human (Anthropos)*, nothing more and
nothing less.

Anthropos means being fully human

When humans allow the Divine
to be in their hearts, to be born,
to grow and take root in them,
then they will be in presence with the
Spirit which will aid them on their
journey to wholeness.
James Galluzzo, *The Spirituality of Mary Magdalene*

19. What does being human look like?

If we embraced our humanity, the world would be at peace, we would live in harmony. There would be no human enemies, there would be no victims or oppressors; we would care for each other. If we made a mistake or hurt someone, we would clean it up right away because other humans would call us back to who we are, to our humanness. Because there would be no need for isolation or abandonment, people would stay connected and not let us disconnect from ourselves or others. We might feel alone or abandoned or misunderstood, but we will be reminded that these are just feelings and that being human is more than just feelings. All humans feel, think, decide and act. So being fully human means using all four functions and honoring that all people have all four functions.

We must have a preferential option for those in need. We are all called to help the oppressed, the victims, the poor and the downtrodden.
Liberation Theology

20. Why hang out with people who don't deserve it?

I came to help people to be connected and to be present to all people, no matter what their struggles or hardships might be. God loves us graciously and extravagantly. And the love is for everyone. Everyone deserves to be loved unconditionally, not only if they are well behaved. This is loving-kindness and it should be our daily practice for ourselves and others, friends and strangers, for those we like and those we do not like.

Reconciliation is to make right,
to heal a broken relationship.
Forgiveness is about our responsibility
to keep our hearts clean. We forgive so
we can have a clean heart and only
then, if the other person is open, can
we repair a broken relationship.
James Galluzzo

21. What is reconciliation?

Reconciliation is about healing broken relationships. It takes two people to come together and be willing to work out whatever has gotten in the way of their connectedness. We have to forgive first, heal our heart, so we can come together in a heart to heart communion.

Holding on to anger and bitterness is like drinking poison and expecting the other person to die.

Buddha Saying

22. What is forgiveness?

Forgiveness is so we can keep our hearts clean. We forgive to have a clean heart. Forgiveness in not dependent on whether the other person says they are sorry or not. If we rely on the other person, we give our power away. If we wait for the other person, we are giving them free rent in our heart. We cannot have a clean heart if we are filled with resentment or bitterness. In letting go of our resentment or bitterness, in the act of forgiving, we are allowing healing to our own hearts.

Wonder:
To see a World in a Grain of Sand
and a Heaven in a Wild Flower,
hold Infinity in the palm of your hand
and Eternity in an hour.
William Blake, *Auguries of Innocence*

23. Why is wonder so important in the teaching?

It is because people struggle, not with belief, but with wonder. We wonder not because we need to explain things or need to fit things into our own system, but we wonder to embrace the beauty and grandeur of the universe. Wonder can bring riches to build a stronger and livelier community. Religion often forgets wonder and awe, and communities do not grow.

We need wonder, delight and beauty to thrive.

We need to find God, and God cannot be found in noise and restlessness.
God is the friend of silence.
See how nature—trees, flowers and grass—grow in silence;
see the stars, the moon and the sun, how they move in silence . . .
We need silence to be able to touch souls.
Mother Teresa

24. Why so much time in Sabbath?

It is in Sabbath that we discover, that we notice, that we see. The good news occurs in silence and quiet. We can see and hear in Sabbath, even the place of unknowing. Unless we make a space for it, we will not hear and see mystery. Be in Sabbath and only if needed, talk. Try to listen in silence. We need to have Sabbath time every day in our lives so we can listen to all that is gracing us.

No matter what they say
It wasn't seven demons
It was seven days
And on the seventh day I knew
I'd know you best and longest
I saw what you could really do
And promised you my deep, deep well,
My meeting mind, my knowing heart
Without my promise, the completing
gift, You knew your work would falter.
I'm angry now and angry then;
I was your true companion.
How could they think you did it all
Without my heart inside you?
Peg Edera

25. Why does Jesus love Mary?

He loves her because of her goodness, for her virtues and for everything that she is. He loves Mary the way God loves him. In Mary, I experience the goodness of God and her goodness dwells in God's love. She reminds me to love. She is a true partner and a leader in our ministry. She will be loved and persecuted because of me, but She will always stay true to her calling.

He is just a man.
And I've had so many men before,
in very many ways.
He is just one more.
Andrew Lloyd Weber, *Jesus Christ Superstar*

26. Why does Jesus not believe in some people being superior to others?

Because, I believe all beings exist in common. There are none more superior or inferior. We are all one, and we are all interconnected. Every person holds God's "isness" and God's "isness" is every person's "isness".

God loves all people equally and fills everyone with divinity, and therefore we should relate to the sacredness of every person. We are called to a connectedness of all beings. There should be no reason to oppress one another, to victimize one another or exploit one another. If we do, we are exploiting God and ourselves.

Humans cannot thrive in a victimized or oppressed state. Equality requires a relationship of respect, reverence, dignity and gratitude. There must be equality and unity for all humans.

This is only possible when we see the divinity in one another.

Human progress is neither automatic nor inevitable . . . every step toward the goal of justice requires sacrifice, suffering, and struggle—the tireless exertions, compassion and passionate concern of dedicated individuals.
Martin Luther King, Jr.

27. Is there a relationship between compassion and justice?

We are called to show compassion and to do justice if we are going to care for creation and treat it well. The just person lives out of their humanity and divinity.

The divine is justice and compassion. Justice and compassion are part of our nature. They are both central to our work in the world.

Where justice is denied, where poverty is enforced, where ignorance prevails and where any one class or religion made to feel that society is an organized conspiracy to oppress, rob and degrade them, neither persons nor property will be safe.
Frederick Douglass

28. Why not correct or put down other religions?

They all have something to teach us; they all have jewels to light the way, and all offer wisdom. There does not have to be a conflict. All paths lead to the sacred and the sacred is in all of them. I never understood why people go to war or kill in the name of religion. Religion should be about peace and justice and not about oppressing groups that come from another tradition.

To the greatest
of the holy priestess
in heaven,
To you I sing.
Inanna, Queen of Heaven and Earth

29. Why has the world lost the feminine presence that once dominated the universe?

In the earliest ages of our history, the power and beauty of the female was as marvelous as the universe. Women brought a balance to the masculine gifts. But when the female (feminine) was beaten down by culture and religion, the masculine part of the population began to fall apart, and their need for control became the bottom line.

The feminine was banished when patriarchal religions ruled and the heart was ignored.

Mary will be one of the many women in history who will work to bring the feminine presence back into balance. It will be a long battle, and she will be ridiculed and misunderstood. She will stand strong and know she is good.

Do not be satisfied with stories, how things have gone with others or institutions. Unfold your own myth: be creative.
Rumi

30. Is this why creativity is lost in so many religions, cultures and institutions?

When we move away from a feminine world dominated by a false sense or limited sense of the masculine, creativity is lost. The power to birth becomes sterile.

So creativity is the passion to make and birth again and again for both women and men.

Creativity rises above restricted concepts of gender. Creativity must be ongoing like a river, perpetual, ongoing like grace, sacred like all beings, and personal. We each must birth the sacred every day. I hope my ministry helps human beings to be born in a divine way.

When we tell our story, we are giving birth. When we listen, we birth one another's story.

The creative births the Sacred.

[Whilst] everything around me is ever changing, ever dying, there is underlying all that change a living power that is changeless, that holds all together, that creates, dissolves and recreates. That informing power or spirit is God . . . and is this power benevolent or malevolent? I see it as purely benevolent. For I can see that in the midst of death, life persists, in the midst of untruth, truth persists, in the midst of darkness, light persists. Hence I gather that God is Life, Truth and Light. God is Love.
God is the supreme Good.

Mahatma Gandhi

31. What is relationship with God?

We all must grow in wisdom and knowledge and learn and live with the truth that God and we are one. We are all one in God. We are God's sons and daughters, and all people are God's children. Relationship with God is a loving relationship, as is our relationships with one another. God is life, truth, light and love.

Often the creative man is motivated by the need to achieve, to beat others, to earn, to be better than, to be successful.
Ann Ryan, *The Transformed Soul*

32. Why do the male disciples have so much trouble embracing the creative, the birthing process and the divine in all people?

As women give birth and create, so the male followers must learn to give birth to their own gifts, their own inherent creativity. Women have to stop taking care of men, or men will never learn. Women can't be only mothers or healers for men, each of us men have our own discoveries to make and our own life to birth. God invites all women and men to the passion of creativity, to do our work, to feel the feelings, to let go of old hurts and fears and to imagine living life like flowing water, like a river that graces, that sanctifies us.

My mother's love has always been a sustaining force for our family, and one of my greatest joys is seeing her integrity, her compassion, her intelligence reflected in my daughters.

Michelle Obama

33. What is the relationship of compassion and the feminine?

Compassion is an inherent human quality found in all men and women. Compassion comes from the word for "womb" in both Hebrew and Arabic. Compassion is an ocean. The Divine holds out compassion in the healing and living water, the sea, the ocean and the rivers.

In the female belongs all water, streams, pools and springs. The female offers living water. The female is grace-filled, living water. This gift of living water, the Divine Feminine, was stripped from the world. From flowing river to "be fruitful and multiply" became the call of women from the patriarchal leaders. The great Mother Earth was limited to one aspect of the Divine Feminine, just as any one aspect or name given to God limits the mystery and fullness of the Sacred.

Compassion is universal but the feminine water image tells us a great deal about compassion. But no one image is enough or complete.

If you're not part of the solution,
you're part of the problem.
Eldridge Cleaver

34. Why does society have such a hard time embracing the message of compassion, peace, justice and love?

It should not be that hard because these are basic qualities and values found in all major religions. These are not foreign ideas to us. But when people get scared, do not clean up old hurts, feel less than or are made to feel unworthy, they lose touch with the core of their humanness. This is why I spend my time talking about the same six messages over and over. It is to remind people that love, compassion, peace, justice, forgiveness and healing are central to their well being and the well being of all the world.

Isolation, ridicule, rejection, abandonment, threats of violence and violence are the big six that get in the way of us being fully human and seeing others as whole and complete.

Charlie Kreiner, *Human Liberation*

35. What are some of the things that have to be overcome to help the good news touch people?

We have to believe that our message is greater than any cultural impediments. The message has to weave through layers of dogma and laws or conditioning based on gender, religion and fear. Our message challenges the cultural norm and confronts moral and philosophical failures.

But we all have to ask ourselves what is our call and how are we making the world a more peaceful and just place for all people. We have to see the privilege and the responsibility of offering a solution of hope for a better world.

I therefore hate the corrupt, slaveholding, women-whipping, cradle-plundering, partial and hypocritical Christianity of the land. . . .I look upon it as the climax of all misnomers, the boldest of all frauds, and the grossest of all libels. Never was there a clearer case of 'stealing the livery of the court of heaven to serve the devil in.' I am filled with unutterable loathing when I contemplate the religious pomp and show, together with the horrible inconsistencies, which everywhere surround me.

Frederick Douglass

36. How can one be part of a community or church that doesn't honor women or that doesn't welcome all people?

A true community of human beings has to be

all-inclusive. There can be no human enemies nor no humans excluded based on race, gender, or religion. All are welcome because all are apart of the human community. Once we separate one group, then others begin to separate a different group and soon there will be no groups left that are honored.

God made this world appear full of variety. We view numerous varieties of scenes around us. What are they?

They are actually various color patterns formed by the reflected seven colors of same light emanated from the same source of light. Moreover, seven different colors of light are also different shades of the SAME ENERGY. So, we view nothing but only LIGHT in the form of various scenes full of variety around us. Similarly, God sent the philosophy of His divine message in various forms full of variety. There are different streams & forms of the same divine MESSAGE emanated from GOD. God made variety, but has given man a brain also to realize the existence of ONE SUPREME POWER i.e. GOD Who manifested Himself in this variety.

37. Does the community hope to create and exist for people like us or is everyone welcome?

The community I hope to build is open to diverse people and groups from all cultural, genders, economic status and ethnicity. We have to hold out that the community needs to learn to be unselfish and practice more thoughtfulness and kindness to those like us and those who are different.

I realized that it's all really one, that John Lennon was correct. We utilize the music to bring down the walls of Berlin, to bring up the force of compassion and forgiveness and kindness between Palestinians and Hebrews. Bring down the walls here in San Diego, Tijuana, Cuba.

Carlos Santana

38. We are so strongly opposed to judging others. How can we overcome our desire to do so?

Judging others is not an inherent human quality.

Does everyone think it is their right to judge other people?

Most of us have enough trouble keeping ourselves on the right track. I guess it is easier to focus on others than to look at the weaknesses in our selves.

I didn't come to judge people, to criticize or blame them; I came to give them the water of healing and show them the way to be responsible and faithful to their own call and to think clearly, relate well and spread good news. This takes compassion and forgiveness for our own mistakes and those of others.

I am surrounded by leaders who repeat incessantly that their kingdom is not of this world, and yet they lay hands on everything they can get.
Napoleon

39. Why get so upset with people who are hypocrites and how do we respond to hypocrites?

It makes me angry when people say one thing and do another.

We have to model our message in words and actions.

It is not enough to speak about love, we must love; it is not enough to preach about forgiveness, we have to practice forgiveness; it is not enough to talk about justice, we have to break down unjust social structures; it is not enough to march for peace, we have to be peacemakers.

Two men went into the temple to pray. One was a Pharisee and the other a tax collector… Jesus said when the two men went home, it was the tax collector and not the Pharisee who was pleasing to God.
Luke 18:14

40. Tell me more about the story of the Pharisee and the tax collector?

We have to be careful about judging either one of them. The Pharisee is a part of his environment and is doing what he was taught by religious leaders. He goes to church, he prays, reads the Bible, avoids "bad" company and believes that God's favor relies on what he does and does not do.

The tax collector is from the lower class; he collected Roman money from the Jewish people and it makes him unclean. He was regarded as a thief.

But the Pharisee is proud and was glad he was not like the tax collector. The tax collector was sorry for what he had done and asked for God's pity. Remember, the tax collector was the one who was pleasing to God. The point of the story is that if we put ourselves above others, we will be put down; but if we humbles ourselves, we will be honored.

Human beings want to be free from oppression, and however long they may agree to stay locked up, to stay oppressed, there will come a time when they say, "That's it!"
Suddenly they find themselves doing something that they never would have thought they would be doing, simply because of the human instinct that makes them turn their face towards freedom.
Aung San Suu Kyi

41. Who are the masses and the little ones mentioned so often?

They are those who are oppressed in any form. They are people who are left out or mistreated. They are the poor, the hungry, the sick, the blind, the lepers, the widows, and the orphans. It is why we have to extend invitations to tax collectors, sinners, prostitutes, and people living in fear and isolation.

Our work is to set people free from any kind of

oppression, free from putting themselves down and putting others down.

This grows out of honoring one's dignity and empowering people to be all they can be.

It is easy enough to be friendly to one's friends. But to befriend the one who regards himself as your enemy is the quintessence of true religion. The other is mere business.
Mahatma Gandhi

42. If we remember that all people are children of the light and are inherently connected to us and to the Divine, then why don't we love all people? And tell me why is it important to love all people?

There were people around for us when we needed light in our own darkness, distress, fear or anxiety and we are called to be a light to others. Others mean not only those who we like but even those we don't.

We don't get to judge people. We don't have to like what they do and we don't even need to like them, but we need to love them.

Inner knowing is seeing with an open kind and loving heart. If we let our heart shut down toward any person, we too are shutting down.
When we shut down we let fear decide for us; we judge, criticize and disconnect.
Loving-kindness is an essential practice.
Buddha Teaching

43. Is this where loving-kindness comes into play in our work?

Yes. As humans we are in need of love and kindness in our lives. We need to practice it for our own self and for others. It is important to daily embrace loving-kindness to ourselves, loving-kindness to those in our lives, loving-kindness to the stranger, loving-kindness to our enemies, loving-kindness to our community and loving-kindness to the whole world. If this is our only daily prayer, it would be a great gift to all.

Let all guests who arrive be received
like Christ, for he is going to say:
I was a stranger and you welcomed me.
(Mt 25:35). ~ Rule of St Benedict 53:1-2 This quote
from Benedict's Rule is a foundational expression of
the principle of hospitality at work: I am called to
welcome in every stranger who comes to the door as
the face of the Divine.

44. What is meant by radical hospitality?

Radical hospitality is inviting our loved ones,
the stranger and our selves into our hearts. Everyone
is a part of our lives as if every cell is a part of our
bodies from the beginning of time. It is not enough
to welcome only those who have been kind to us.
We must offer unconditional hospitality. This can
only take place if we stop judging others or seeing
ourselves as better than others. None of us are
without struggles and fears. We have all been hurt.

God wants us to know that life is a journey of learning, of growing in wisdom and knowledge. Our stories are ongoing processes, and when we include love and compassion we will see that we are enough.
James Galluzzo

45. So many religions call us to be perfect. Why not call us to be perfect?

I do not call people to be perfect because that would set all up for failure. We would never be worthy. We are not called to be perfect; we are called to be human, and that is enough work for us to focus on. Adam and Eve had paradise but they wanted more, they wanted to eat the tree of knowledge.

So many people fight to be successful and then they think they are better than and can use power over others. They ignore their own humanity and the humanity of the people they are controlling or putting down.

The call to be perfect is a power play by

religions to make sure that people never are successful and therefore never enough. It sets up a codependent relationship with religion.

The earth will not continue to offer its harvest, except with faithful stewardship. We cannot say we love the land and then take steps to destroy it or prevent it from being used by future generations.

Pope John Paul II

46. What does it mean to be stewards of the earth?

The world was created as a sign of the wonders of creation. It is often in the beauty of creation that we find the Sacred. Creation is a gift for all people for all times and it is our responsibility and privilege to be good stewards of the earth. The earth helps us to discover the cosmic story and the grandeur of the universe.

Why would we want to waste the earth's resources, destroy the beauty that has been given to us or hoard the resources out of greed?

Enough is the food for a banquet. There is no need for self-hunger. Each moment is where you are in present time and that is enough for now.
Dalai Lama

47. Why is all the talk about not being enough false?

Not being enough is one of the greatest mistakes that keep us from being all we can be. The "not enough" message blocks creativity, risk taking, being prophetic and sabotages our true self.

We are enough, in the good times and the hard times. We might not feel that we are enough, but that is only a feeling. The reality is we are enough.

What should young people do with their lives today? Many things, obviously. But the most daring thing is to create stable communities in which the terrible disease of loneliness can be cured.

Kurt Vonnegut

48. Why is community so important?

We cannot live and do the work of peace and justice alone. We need one another to build a sense of belonging and to discover our deep connection. Community might not be efficient and can be messy; but if we want everyone to be a part, then we have to make time to listen, to hear differences, to honor diversity and to help each other know that we are never alone.

Each of us has a story to tell, a light to shine, and if that doesn't happen the rest of us lose out. No one can tell another person's story or shine another person's light.

*God is known only when . . .
apprehended as unknown, and heard
only when we realize that we do not
know the sound of God's voice. The
words God utters are words full of
silence and they are bait to draw us
into silence.*

Thomas Merton

49. Tell me again why silence is so important?

If we are to grow in wisdom and knowledge, our greatest asset will be silence. Silence is where we discover, see, wonder and find the Sacred. It will be our greatest work to help people create the space to be silent. The world is full of distraction from everyday needs, worries and anxieties to problems in community, churches and temples and in the larger world.

Silence is when we sit quietly, rest in the garden, go to the desert or are held by another. It is amazing how much we learn when we are together or just sitting quietly with others.

This will be a challenge for the followers to

explain to others, especially our male disciples. They are busy and active and do not make the time to sit quietly or have the time to reflect. When I ask them to sit with me, they fall asleep. They will never be able to truly grasp our message until they can sit with it in silence.

[Christ] was born of a virgin, that we might be born of God. He took our flesh that He might give us His Spirit. He lay in the manger that we might lie in paradise. He came down from heaven, that He might bring us to heaven. And what was all this but love? If our hearts be not rocks, this love of Christ should affect us. Behold love that surpasses knowledge.

(Eph. 3:19) - *A Body of Divinity,* pg. 196

50. Why do others make up stories about the virgin birth?

Remember, it is just a story. People need me to be special, to be a hero. They need me to fit in the culture of the time. Isis, along with many other famous goddesses, were said to have had a virgin birth. It is the way of making me famous and above others, but I am fully human and was born of Mary and Joseph and discovered my deep connection to the Divine throughout my life.

Remember we teach through stories, myths and parables. Stay focused on the core truths.

To enjoy good health, to bring true happiness to one's family, to bring peace to all, one must first discipline and control one's own mind. If a man can control his mind, he can find the way to Enlightenment, and all wisdom and virtue will naturally come to him.
Buddha Saying

51. What does it mean, "those who have a mind to understand, let them understand" or "those who have ears, let them hear" or "those who have eyes to see, let them see"?

We all have a mind, let us use it; we must open our minds to understand, to be all we can be without limits. Human nature is limitless.

We all have ears and eyes to stay connected, to follow our hearts, be open, to listen and hear the good news in everyone's stories.

Who do people say I am?

52. Jesus, people say you are a revolutionary, a radical, a teacher, a prophet, a lawbreaker, the Son of Man, the Son of God, a carpenter or a heretic. Who are you?

I am a human being who preaches and lives out of love, compassion, justice, peace, healing and forgiveness. I tried to be good, gentle, kind, loving and thoughtful. I want to be known as a teacher who spreads the good news and give hope to all and to treat people with respect and dignity.

❧ REFERENCES TO HER BOOK ON THE QUESTIONS ❧

(*Panarion*, Chapter 26)

In early Christian history, the **Panarion** is called *Adversus Haereses* (Latin: "Against Heresies.") It was written in Greek beginning in 374 or 375 and gives important information on the Jewish Gospels.

Regarding the Questions of Mary the following addresses the book:

8:1 they published certain *Questions of Mary.*

8:2 for in the so-called 'Greater Questions of Mary'—there are also 'Lesser' ones—they claim that Jesus reveals it to her after taking her to the mountain to pray.

8.6 There is little to say concerning the 'Lesser Questions of Mary' mentioned here, although some have attempted to identify it with otherwise known texts (such as the Pistis Sophia or the Gospel of Mary).

James Galluzzo has been a spiritual director and guide for 25 years, working with individuals, teaching classes, and giving retreats. He is an artist, author, priest, teacher, administrator, diversity trainer, and spiritual director.

Fr. Galluzzo is the author of: *The Spirituality of Mary Magdalene, A Spiritual Handbook: A Resource for Travelers and Guides on the Journey, Jesus as Liberator and the Gospel Values, Quotes and Reflection Questions for Journaling your Spiritual Journey, Spiritual Writing: Be the Author of Your Own Story, and Stop Whining, Choose Life.* His original artwork is displayed with reflections on *The Sacred Feminine, Sacred Masculine* and *The Merge* in *The New Eden Series.*

He founded Allies: People to People, an organization that teaches a way of living and thinking that honors human liberation based on the Gospel values, and that works to end oppression of any kind: sexism, racism, classism, ageism, adultism, and homophobia.

Fr. Galluzzo is the director of the non-profit organization, Diversity as Gift that works to honor all and teach about dignity from a spiritual perspective. He is also the director of the Urban Spirituality Center in Portland, Oregon.

He holds a BA degree from Gonzaga University, an MAT degree from Reed College, an

Administrative Certificate from Lewis and Clark College, an MA degree in Theology from Catholic University of America, Mount Angel Seminary, and Portland State University.

Fr. Galluzzo leads workshops throughout the country on Conflict Resolution, Community Building, Diversity, Gospel Values, Spirituality, and Human Liberation.

Marianne Manning has had broad experience as a high school art teacher, community art teacher, and Artist in Schools. She became a full time painter five years ago. Marianne continues to refine her art by taking workshops from some of the top artists in the world. She has been a member of the portrait society of America for the past five years.

She recently had a wonderful show at the Juneau/Douglas City Museum. One of her paintings was published in the 2015 edition of *Title Echoes*, a literary and art journal showcasing the art and writing of Southeast Alaskans.

Marianne was thrilled to be asked to paint Mary Magdalene for the cover of this book. She named one of her daughters after this wonderful saint.

She is available to do portraits.

Other examples of her work are available on her website: mariannemanningstudio.com